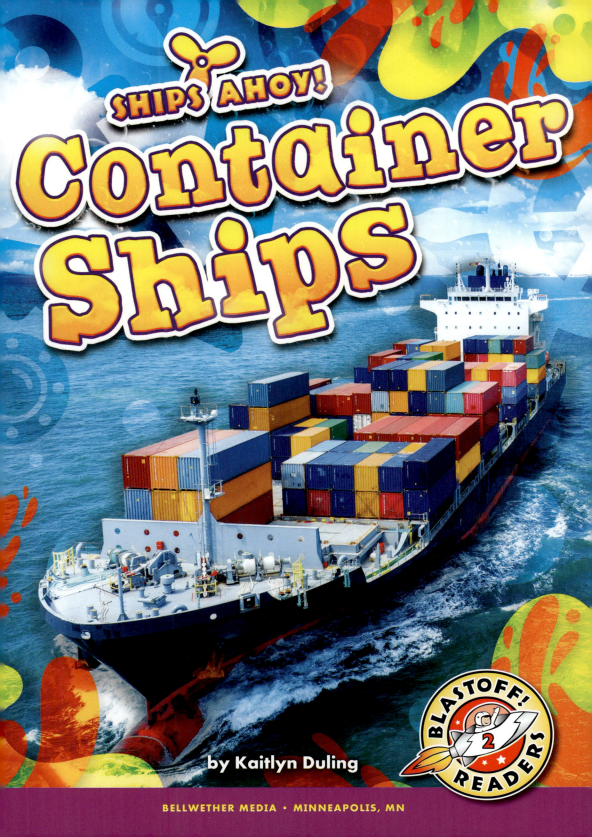

 **Blastoff! Readers** are carefully developed by literacy experts to build reading stamina and move students toward fluency by combining standards-based content with developmentally appropriate text.

 Level 1 provides the most support through repetition of high-frequency words, light text, predictable sentence patterns, and strong visual support.

 Level 2 offers early readers a bit more challenge through varied sentences, increased text load, and text-supportive special features.

 Level 3 advances early-fluent readers toward fluency through increased text load, less reliance on photos, advancing concepts, longer sentences, and more complex special features.

★ **Blastoff! Universe**

This edition first published in 2026 by Bellwether Media, Inc.

No part of this publication may be reproduced in whole or in part without written permission of the publisher. For information regarding permission, write to Bellwether Media, Inc., Attention: Permissions Department, 3500 American Blvd W, Suite 150, Bloomington, MN 55431.

Library of Congress Cataloging-in-Publication Data

LC record for Container Ships available at: https://lccn.loc.gov/2025010690

Text copyright © 2026 by Bellwether Media, Inc. BLASTOFF! READERS and associated logos are trademarks and/or registered trademarks of Bellwether Media, Inc. Bellwether Media is a division of FlutterBee Education Group.

Editor: Suzane Nguyen   Designer: Jeffrey Kollock

Printed in the United States of America, North Mankato, MN.

Table of Contents

What Are Container Ships?	4
World Travelers	12
Go, Go Cargo!	20
Glossary	22
To Learn More	23
Index	24

What Are Container Ships?

cargo

Container ships are large ships. They carry **cargo**.

Cargo is stored in big boxes called **containers**. Ships move containers from **port** to port!

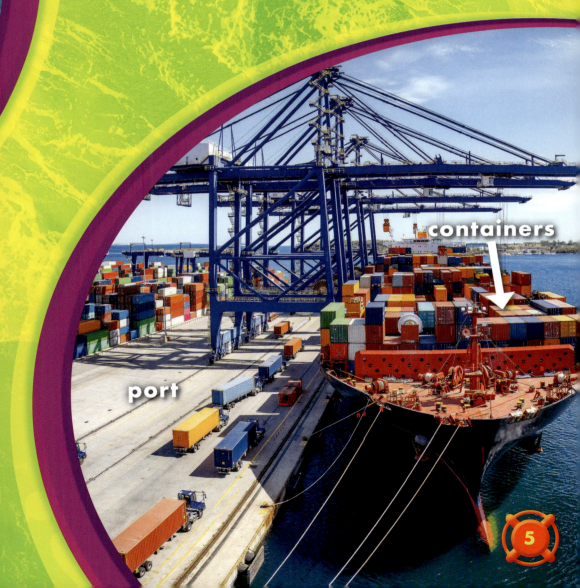

These ships are long and flat. Containers are stacked on the ship's **deck**.

Parts of a Container Ship

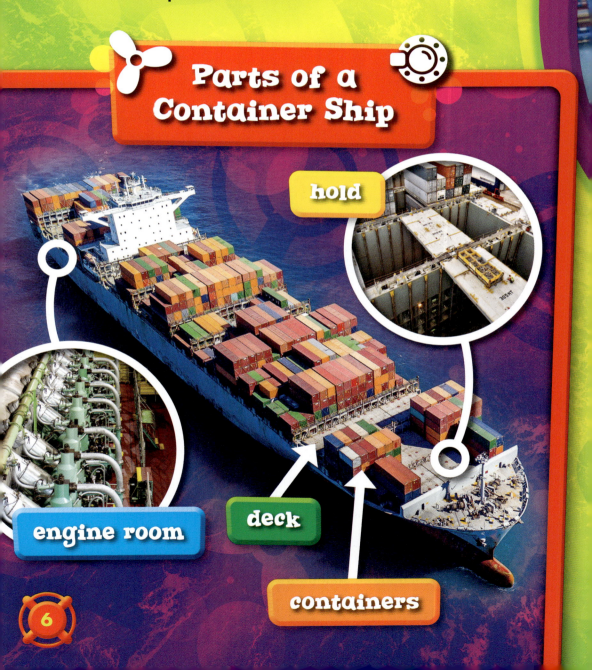

hold

engine room

deck

containers

The **hold** also stores containers.

The ships are powered by large **engines**. Engines are found in the engine room.

The engines send power to the ship's **propellers**.

propeller

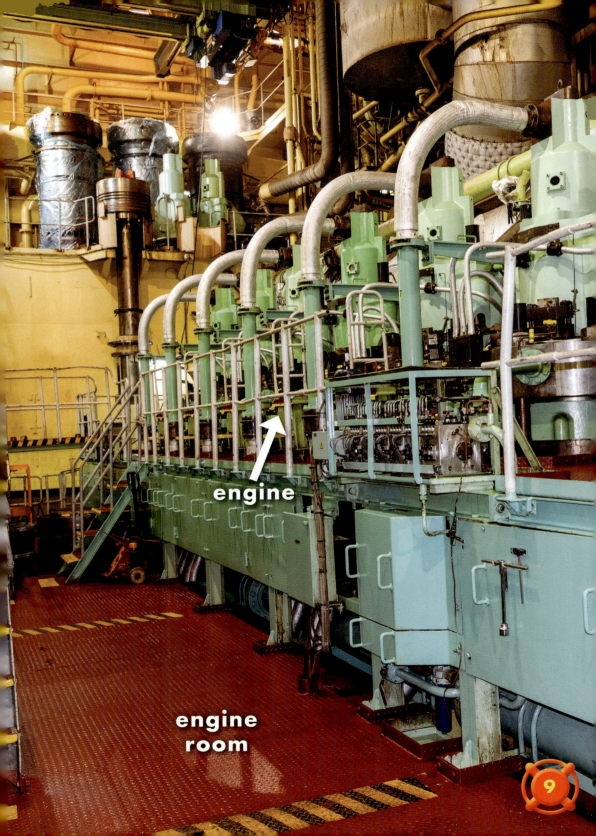

Types of Container Ships

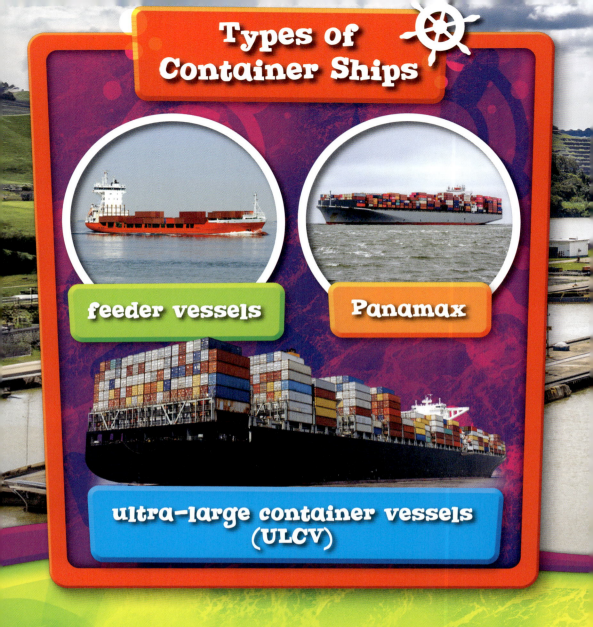

feeder vessels

Panamax

ultra-large container vessels (ULCV)

Feeder vessels are small container ships. They move containers from ports to bigger ships.

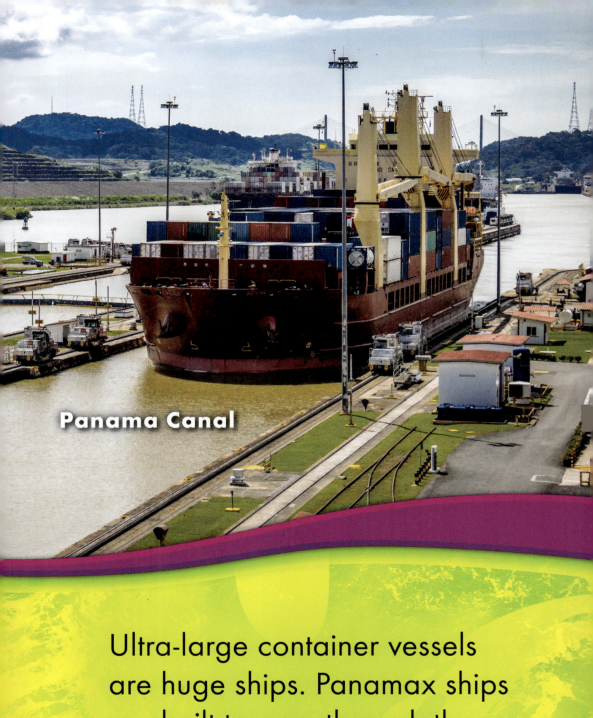

Panama Canal

Ultra-large container vessels are huge ships. Panamax ships are built to pass through the **Panama Canal**.

World Travelers

↑ captain

engineers

Container ships can carry around 20 workers. Captains sail and keep the ship safe.

Engineers make sure parts work smoothly.

Ship Stats

MSC Loreto

Size: 1,312 feet (399.9 meters) long; 201.1 feet (61.3 meters) wide

Type: ultra-large container vessel (ULCV)

Speed: 22.5 knots (26 miles or 41.7 kilometers per hour)

Purpose: can move 24,000 containers at once

Thousands of people work at each port. Cargo handlers load and unload ships.

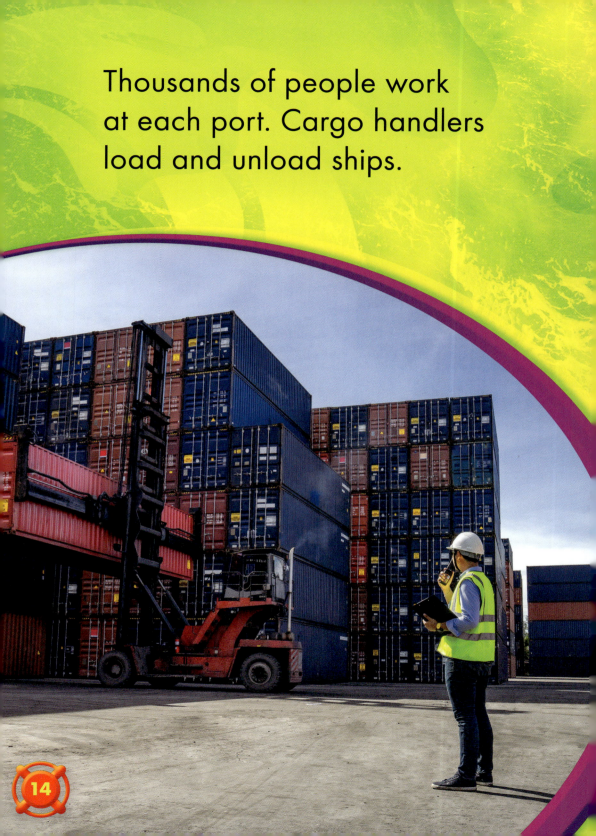

crane

Containers are heavy! Workers use **cranes** to lift and move containers.

Containers must be the same size and shape when being stacked.

Trains, trucks, and ships all carry containers!

Loading a Container Ship

1

A truck or train brings the containers to the port.

2

A special cart brings the containers close to the ship.

3

A crane lifts the containers onto the ship.

4

Workers add bars and chains to keep the containers in place.

Businesses use container ships to move cargo around the world.

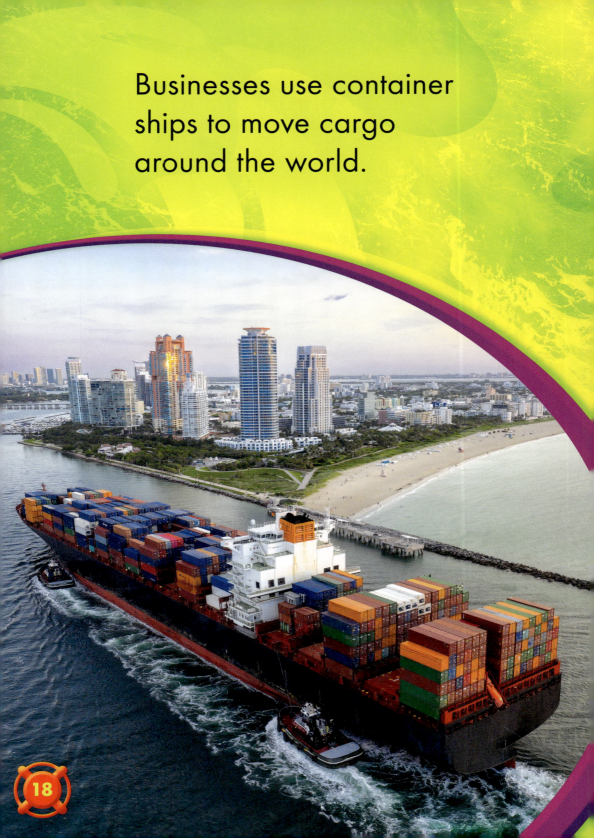

Container ships sail on oceans and through canals. They travel around 24 **knots** (27.6 miles or 44.4 kilometers per hour).

Go, Go Cargo!

Without container ships, it would be harder to get things like clothes, food, and more.

These big ships bring us what we need!

Glossary

cargo—goods carried by a ship

containers—large boxes that hold goods

cranes—machines used to lift and move heavy loads

deck—the flat part on the top of a ship

engineers—people who design engines, computers, and other machines

engines—machines with moving parts that change power into motion

hold—a large area below a ship's deck that is used to store cargo

knots—units of measurement used to explain the speed of a ship

Panama Canal—a human-made waterway that connects the Atlantic and Pacific Oceans; canals allow boats to pass from one body of water to another.

port—a place where ships are loaded and unloaded

propellers—parts of a ship that have blades that spin; propellers help a ship move through water.

To Learn More

AT THE LIBRARY

Linn, Margo. *Every Here Has A There: Moving Cargo by Container Ship*. Watertown, Mass.: Charlesbridge, 2024.

Rathburn, Betsy. *A Ship's Day*. Minneapolis, Minn.: Bellwether Media, 2024.

Schmitt, Kelly Rice. *I Ship: A Container Ship's Colossal Journey*. Minneapolis, Minn.: Millbrook Press, 2023.

ON THE WEB

Factsurfer.com gives you a safe, fun way to find more information.

1. Go to www.factsurfer.com.

2. Enter "container ships" into the search box and click 🔍.

3. Select your book cover to see a list of related content.

Index

businesses, 18
canals, 19
captains, 12
cargo, 4, 5, 18
cargo handlers, 14
containers, 5, 6, 7, 10, 15, 16, 17
cranes, 15
deck, 6, 7
engine room, 8, 9
engineers, 12, 13
engines, 8, 9
feeder vessels, 10
hold, 7
load, 14, 17
MSC *Loreto*, 13
oceans, 19
Panama Canal, 11
Panamax ships, 11
parts of a container ship, 6
port, 5, 10, 14
propellers, 8
speed, 19

trains, 17
trucks, 17
types, 10
ultra-large container vessels, 11
workers, 12, 15

The images in this book are reproduced through the courtesy of: GreenOak, front cover, pp. 1, 17 (4); Federico Rostagno, p. 3; moofushi, p. 4; Sven Hansche, pp. 5, 21; AurelioaPhoto, p. 6; donvictori0, pp. 6 (hold), 7 (inset); Mariusz Bugno, pp. 6 (engine room), 9; APchanel, p. 7; Angelika Bentin, p. 8; Jamie, p. 10 (feeder vessels); mark stephens photography, p. 10 (Panamax); StockStudio Aerials, p. 10 (ULCV); diegograndi, p. 11; LEONARDO VITI, p. 12; Chris Pearsall/ Alamy Stock Photo, p. 12 (inset); PA Images/ Alamy Stock Photo, p. 13; ibravery, p. 14; Kalyakan, pp. 15, 20; Elles Rijsdijk, p. 16; furuoda, p. 17 (1); Pawinee, p. 17 (2); ake1150, p. 17 (3); Zenstratus, p. 18; Yellow Boat, p. 19; newroadboy, p. 23.